THE SIMPLE ACT OF SELF PUBLISHING WITH AMAZON

A SIMPLE STEP BY STEP GUIDE

GEORGIANNE LANDY-KORDIS

THE SIMPLE ACT

OF

SELF PUBLISHING

WITH AMAZON

Prepared for publication by FIA/Films by Independent Artists, Inc., dba LilyHeart Publishing, Oklahoma.

Printed in the United States of America

ABOUT THIS BOOK

This book is about how you as an individual with whatever amount of education, can step-by-step publish your very own book with Amazon. That book or books that you've spent so much time and passion on. I know because I have done it and I continue to publish my very own books.

You must be at least 18 to open your own account with Amazon or have a parent or guardian open one for you.

I have purchased several books for such information and have to tell you, many have a lot of blah, blah, blah before they give you what you are looking for and also throughout the book.

This is the only blah, blah, blah you will have to hear.

I will say, I can only tell you what I have learned and used/use and hope that it helps you and/or perhaps takes you to more areas that may lead you to find even more and better ways to publish your books.

Also, *I* do so much better when I see examples, so have added examples of my own works to help you.

GET BUSY

If you haven't already...write your book. Something you are passionate about.

It can be in Microsoft Word Document if that's what you prefer as you write. It's the only program I use.

When finished, proof read. You can proof read it yourself over and over again but you should get a friend or two to help because you can always miss something. You can always hire an editor also. Some charge $10.00 - $25.00 per hour...some say they charge about $4.00 per page.

I cannot express enough how important it is to have correct spelling and to be grammatically correct. Reviewers *will* point out your flaws.

TO INCORPORATE OR NOT

If you plan on making this sort of a business for yourself and want to keep expenses and earnings separate from your personal income, etc., you can set up an S Corporation. Simple...go to your state site to incorporate. If you type in, "how to incorporate in (*your state*), many sites offer their help but I think it is best to go to your states official site. It's just a matter of filling out a form and I think it costs about $50.00, if that. You do not have to hire a lawyer etc. If you will be sole owner, that's ok. You could have officers but not necessary.

You can always change things later if need, depending on how rich you get!

If you set up a corporation or not, you can still set up a separate account at a bank for your earnings to go directly to, from your book sales. Whatever you choose, but have a plan before you set up an account with kdp amazon publishing.

COPYRIGHT YOUR WORK

Next….Copyright your work. Go to www.copyright.gov. Click on registration portal, next click on home, (it's tiny at the top left) then register. You will register under Literary Works unless you write screenplays, then you would register under Performing Arts. You will send them a pdf file copy of your work. The cost is $35.00 (pdf –Portal Document File)

When you get ready to type up/create your copyright page, you will be able to create the copyright symbol © by holding the ALT key down and type 0169…let go and it appears!

The copyright office will send you a copy of your registered work. You do not have to wait for your copy before publishing. Confirmation should come in your email that you used to register your work. Yes, you can send paper copies into the copyright office but why spend money on all those pieces of paper and postage etc., to do that. So much cheaper and easier to send them the pdf file.

FORMATING

Select a book size. 6 x 9 is a good size.

If your manuscript/book is in word document, I would copy to have an extra copy or two. You might just need them. You will need one for your kindle version because of the formatting difference.

Then set your size. Go to page layout and select size then pick the correct size. You may have to click on more sizes which pulls up page layout and then put in 6" width and 9" length or whatever size you choose. Yes, you want "whole document" and then click OK. You will want to insert page numbers and then you have to check each page to make sure everything is spaced and flowing correctly as in turning pages of an actual book. Most books as you know, place the numbers at the bottom and centered.

I mainly write screenplays so spacing and margins are different than books, especially for E-readers. It takes more work but for those interested in publishing their screenplay, I will go over it later in this book.

You will want a title page first of course. It should show up on the left once you have changed your size. Then insert a blank page so your title page will have a blank back. Look at some book title pages, if you'd like or need to. You will want the title in larger print first.

Then your copyright etc., page should also show up on the left side/facing page as well. Center the following information:

And I Thought
I'd be a
Nun

Georgianne Landy-Kordis

Your next page should list the following information. You will be assigned an ISBN # from Amazon/KDP when you get ready to publish. They walk you through the process step by step. (ISBN – International Standard Book Number) Every book has its own identifying number.

The only thing here is that you will have to type in your ISBN Number to your copyright page AFTER you start the publishing process because you do not get one assigned until you start the process.

Example of Copyright page:

And I Thought I'd be a Nun

Copyright © 2014
Georgianne Landy-Kordis
All rights reserved.

ISBN-13: 978-1499674262 ISBN-10: 1499674260

Scripture quotations are from the HOLY BIBLE, NEW INTERNATIONAL VERSION®. Copyright 1973, 1978, 1984 Biblica. Used by permission of Zondervan. All rights reserved.

This book is available in print at most online retailers.

Published by LilyHeart Publishing Piedmont, Oklahoma

Prepared for publication by: www.40daypublishing.com
Oklahoma City, Oklahoma

Re-edited by Cindy Jolls Kahland May, 2018

Cover design by Jonna Feavel
Author photo by Photography by Jonna

Published in the United States of America

This book has two ISBN #'s but I believe now that most only receive one number especially through kdp publishing.

I mainly write screenplays but my memoir was great therapy for me. So here is another example of one of my screenplays I have put in book form as well.

Another example of Title Page:

GOLDSBY

BUFFALO SOLDIER

A SCREENPLAY

BASED ON

FRED STAFF'S NOVEL

SERGEANT GOLDSBY

AND THE 10TH CAVALRY

GEORGIANNE LANDY-KORDIS

And the next page, copyright page example:

GOLDSBY – BUFFALO SOLDIER

I have no pictures on my title pages for my screenplays but feel free to if you want.

My memoir was my first published book and I paid a hefty price to have them do what I am telling you right now in this little book. Mainly because I thought I couldn't do it even after reading their book. After that, I learned how to do it myself.

Insert another blank page after your copyright page so it has a blank back as well.

If you have a Table of Content page, it too should start on the left/ facing page. If your Table of Contents runs more than one page, it's ok to let it continue on the back side of the first page.

Your book should follow and then again, start on the left/facing page.

At the end of your book you might need to insert one more blank page for your Author Page as it should also be a facing page. Preferably on the right side of the last page of your book.

Your author page could look something like this:

ABOUT THE AUTHOR

Georgianne Landy-Kordis studied screenwriting and directing at the University of Oklahoma. She has written, directed and produced promotional scripts as well as worked as a videographer through her own company, FIA/Films by Independent Artists, Inc. She is inspired to write human interest stories and offer emotional insight. She is happily married to Kenneth, loving their little Shih Tzu's and cattle ranching in Oklahoma. Her daughter is happily married and her teenage granddaughter is writing her first novel.

(This author page mentions my daughter because people would want to know after reading my memoir...and I mentioned my granddaughter because I think she is a great writer and will one day finish one of her many books that she has started)

SET UP YOUR ACCOUNT

Now you can go to https://kdp.amazon.com

There used to be "createspace" for paperback books and the kdp was for E-books, but now there is only the Kindle Direct for both paperback and E-book publications and it's free. Yes FREE and you own the rights to your book.

On the left hand side you will find where you can create an account and also manage your account. You will set up bank account information so your royalties can go directly to your bank account. They pay quarterly. If you set up accounts with other distributors they may pay differently.

They also have in the same column, helpful steps on preparing, publishing and promoting and managing your books. And you can also check important information such as, sales, royalties, how you get paid and tax information from that same column. There is also some legal information there as well.

You will notice, "author copies." This is where you can purchase books that you want to give away, have book signings with or even donate to your local library. These copies can be purchased by you at a cheaper rate.

And finally on the left side, they have, "contact us". They are very helpful. You can e-mail them or I always asked them to call me because I wanted help and answers right away. They will gladly walk you through any problem you might be having or any questions you need answered.

I think everything you need is on the left side of the home page, but they also have listed a Step-by-step guide, Learn on your own and frequently asked questions. You should read and explore anything and/or everything they have to show you.

When you have a book or books published through kdp, just go to the top of the home page and click on Bookshelf to look at your books and Reports, to see if any books have sold.

STEP BY STEP GUIDE

After you have an account set up, you can proceed with their simple step-by-step guide.

It will ask you to create a cover. They have samples you can pick from and choose one of theirs. It will have your title, author name etc., or you can upload one of your own pics and they will show you how it will look with title, etc. If you don't like what they show you or you don't have a cover pic for your book, there are places on the internet that you can find one to your liking. The ones that say they are free might be but there are also some that charge a small fee. They also ask that you credit the pic. Do this on your copyright page toward the bottom.

EXAMPLE:

A Kindled Affair

Cover: istock – credit: inarik

Prepared for publication by: FIA/Films by Independent Artists, Inc., dba LilyHeart Publishing, Oklahoma

www.georgiannelandy-kordis.com

Printed in the United States of America

IMAGES AND PHOTOGRAPHS

The pic of LilyHeart Publishing heart is my company logo. I had a local girl do the artwork of something I had in my mind. She did a great job. I have made this a business because I plan on publishing my granddaughters' books or anyone else who would like my help.

Images and photographs must be high resolution. At least 300 dpi or higher. (dpi – dots per inch) kdp amazon will let you know if your images will work or not. Sometimes it's a matter of resizing.

If you are using any images or photographs within the book itself, you must own the rights to use them.

Always keep in mind there are copyright laws on pictures/images. I went to one site and out of the six pictures I chose, the site showed me that one had no copyright restrictions. So that's the one I used. I have also purchased an image for my books and one of my books a friend provided props for and I took a jillion' pics of it till I found the perfect one for my book. Kdp allows you to upload your own pic also for your cover.

When you have a cover you want to use, upload it to kdp. They will show you a sample. You can change it as many times as you need. Also remember there is a back to your cover. They indicate places for an author photo if you'd like and description of book, etc. There is also a blank square for the barcode for which they will add once your cover is complete. Look at other books to give you an idea what to add to the back of your cover. Here again if you use an author photo make sure it is of high resolution and that you have the rights. Sometimes if taken by a photographer, you may need to get their permission.

Here are a few places you can find pics for your cover(s).

Dreamtime.com
Picsart.com
Istock.com
123rf.com

There are probably more, check the internet. There are also places you can get creative with your own photos.

This is the cover I came up with when using my friends' props.

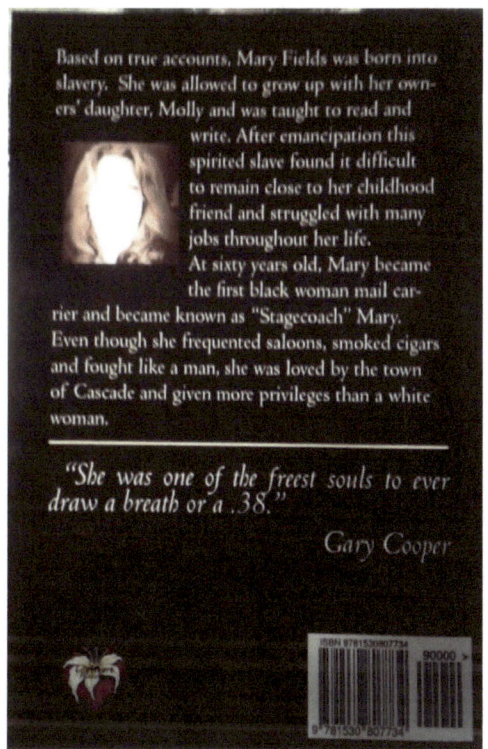

Based on true accounts, Mary Fields was born into slavery. She was allowed to grow up with her owners' daughter, Molly and was taught to read and write. After emancipation this spirited slave found it difficult to remain close to her childhood friend and struggled with many jobs throughout her life.

At sixty years old, Mary became the first black woman mail carrier and became known as "Stagecoach" Mary. Even though she frequented saloons, smoked cigars and fought like a man, she was loved by the town of Cascade and given more privileges than a white woman.

"She was one of the freest souls to ever draw a breath or a .38."

Gary Cooper

This is a sample of what you can put on your back cover.

UPLOAD YOUR MANUSCRIPT

After you have figured out your cover, text, photo and back cover information you should check and recheck it. Approve it when ready. As I said, you can change it as many times as you need to. You can even change it after it has been published. Only problem is, it will take it a couple of days before it is available for sale again.

You can even reload new text after your book has been published, in case you found some mistake. There again, it will take a couple of days before available again to the public. But....not a bad deal at all. Kind of takes some pressure off the whole process.

The next step will be to upload your book. They ask for a pdf file.

It takes a few minutes for it to upload the book. It will ask you to check your work. You can review it virtually right then. You can also ask for a hard copy to be sent to your home address. I always check it virtually. It's a matter of turning page by page, checking for text starting on the right pages, check to see if text falls within the margins, etc. Check for everything you can think of. Approve it and you are done. Don't freak out, like I said if you find you need to change anything, you can. You just need to go through the process again.

Once you have your paperback book approved, they will ask if you would like to process a kindle version. Of course you do.

They will walk you through this process also.

Some people may choose a different cover for the E-reader book. If so, then you will need to upload the different cover for the kindle version. I actually had to resize one of the pics I had for my paperback book before it could be approved because of the resolution but it would work for my kindle version, so I had to upload the pic again only a smaller resized version.

They can transfer your text that you had uploaded for your paperback book directly to the kindle version. Here again, you need to really look at those pages. I always check the tablet version as well as phone and kindle and if they all look pretty good then I approve it. They will never be perfectly formatted as you know for E-readers but make sure it looks the best it can.

FORMAT E-READER FOR SCREENPLAYS

As I mentioned before, I mainly write & publish screenplays and if you do the same, formatting for the E-readers is a little more complicated.

First you'll need to highlight your screenplay and then go to the setting "no spacing". Also you may have to re-tab your character names over the dialogue as well as the dialogue. And do not have two spaces after a period...only one.

Also no page numbering is necessary for E-readers.

After you upload, make sure to do the virtual viewing. Kdp will allow you to view how it will look on a kindle, tablet and phone. Remember that E-readers will never be perfect fit or spacing, but make sure you check each page to see if all is looking good.

PRICING, ETC.

Next, Amazon allows you to select your retail price and it will show you what your royalty pays in several countries, provided you sell in several areas.

You can also select kindle direct for higher payments and there are also opportunities to give your book away free for a few days or offer a price promotion.

Explore all you can on the site, see how you can profit from all that they have to offer.

Here's the site again.

https://kdp.amazon.com

MARKETING

Continuing on with the step-by-step guide, Amazon allows you to choose categories that your book falls into and pick an age range. They also allow you to come up with words or phrases that relate to your book. All of these things help people locate your type of books.

As far as further marketing; you as a self publisher...well there are many books and sites for that subject. You will have to explore to find the many, many ways you can market yourself. You may also want to develop your own website and either use your Facebook page to promote yourself or have a Facebook author page. And, maybe you are a twitter kind of person.

CONCLUSION

Writing is a labor of love. Completing a book can be exciting and possibly a little scary but when finished take a deep breath, be proud and take the next big step.

Publishing your work is exhilarating. Nothing like having your book in your hands...a published author!

I hope this book has been easy enough to follow and has helped you to accomplish the act of self-publishing. Soon you will get the hang of the process and the more you do, the easier it gets.

Thank you for taking the time to read this book. I have tried my best to cover steps in a way you could follow. If you have found this process useful, please let me know by leaving a review on Amazon. I do read them and care that I have been helpful for inspiring authors accomplish their dreams.

If you run across a problem or have additional questions or just need some inspiration, feel free to visit my web site, and leave a message. www.georgiannelandy-kordis.com

GOOD LUCK!

HAPPY WRITING & HAPPY PUBLISHING, AUTHOR !!